I0756258

FINISHING LINE PRESS
www.finishinglinepress.com

THE TOWN HALL CLOCK

poems by

Francis O'Brien

Finishing Line Press
Georgetown, Kentucky

THE TOWN HALL CLOCK

For Judith, who keeps the lights on at O'Brien's after 150 years

ISBN 979-8-89990-457-8 First Edition

ACKNOWLEDGMENTS

"Trainland" and "Small Town Sunrise" to Poetry Society of Michigan

Publisher: Leah Huete de Maines
Editor: Christen Kincaid
Cover Art: Francis O'Brien
Author Photo: Kelley Whitman
Cover Design: Elizabeth Maines McCleavy

Order online: www.finishinglinepress.com
also available on amazon.com

Author inquiries and mail orders:
Finishing Line Press
PO Box 1626
Georgetown, Kentucky 40324
USA

Contents

Under The Town Hall Clock

a small boy kissing a row of statues
knowing that as soon as the light went out
a giant yellow cyclops eye would be peering in his window
and that on each hour, Quasimodo would be
working his biceps on the bell ropes

after the hardest shift was done at day change
and before the easy start to the new one,
pirates would storm The Square shouting and swearing
and sometimes exchanging blows

that would be the last sound
until the first crow found a discarded chip bag
or the fruit pickers assembled for Lambs' lorries
and the shirt factory women flocked for first shift

on Fridays you would hear a wooden push cart
rattle unsteadily over the pavements before being
put in place by a man in a long brown trench coat
for the Moore Street smoked cod sellers

after seven, the town rolling over for another rest
until the bells built up to higher numbers and you
wondered if Kai Moore had a hunch under that trench coat
and if he was the one that pulled the ropes
inside the Town Hall clock

The Mahogany

they tended shop for all their lives
though more they could have done
and all were happy men and leaders in their time
their mark was honesty and
they were always known for
an open ear and a giving hand
their pleasure was in the simple things
and never stirring far afield
the world, it seems, was glad to come to greet them there
standing counter-side

and now eleven decades on
another stands shop side
to that mahogany
wondering whether it too
will shape his destiny

Forty Types of Rain

1. that which falls straight down on your head
2. the one that sweeps in from the side in the West
3. that which is close to hail and pings your checks
4. the sort that disguises itself as a light sweat
5. the invisible one you only recognize after you've found that you're damp
6. that which is constipated inside grey clouds giving you headaches
7. the one that angry gods throw on us in thunder
8. the rain of complaints over the lack of it
9. the sort that gets inside your coat when you ride a bicycle
10. mist
11. the one that makes all the noise on your windows
12. the sort that imitates cats running on a galvanized roof
13. that which tap dances sporadically in puddles
14. the sort that flushes down suddenly like a toilet and then goes silent
15. that which falls on one side of the stage while the sun shines on the other
16. the sort that menaces in black clouds around the mountain but doesn't fall
17. that which is hard enough to bounce up from concrete
18. the kind that coagulates on leaves in blobs but doesn't seem to fall on humans
19. the hypnotic rhythmic sort that falls all night sending you deeper into sleep
20. the kind that lashes at irregular intervals across the side of the house
21. the transgender stuff that can't decide if it's sleet
22. freezing rain
23. the wall of moisture that seems not to be broken into drops
24. the sort different people call "downpour"
25. that which exists permanently on the top of certain mountains
26. the kind that's heavier than mist but lighter than fog
27. that which changes direction like a spray painter to make sure it wets all of you
28. the kind that when donkeys know it's coming turn their heads towards the wall
29. that which brings a ceiling down on your world for days
30. the type that in summer seems to rise back up again as soon as it falls
31. that which on the shoreline mixes with sea foam and forms a salty layer on your face
32. drizzle
33. the teasing kind that comes in summer showers
34. "Spring rain" (whatever that might be to you)

35. the type that falls when it should be snowing or before it turns to snow
36. that which seems to chase the melting snow making a cacophony of drain-filling noises
37. the sort that fools you when you head out for a walk and return drenched from
38. the "sociable" type that the forecasters says will come "mixed with snow"
39. that which different people refer to as "pissing down outside"
40. the kind the coatless Irish simply refuse to recognize is falling at all

A Mother Knows Best

at fifty my back went somewhere it shouldn't
have : into pain-without warning or cause-
physical therapy helped where the doctor couldn't
with endless hours humping Swiss balls

two years later I looked down to find
my left and right in symmetry at ten past ten
the configuration Mother had so long despised
and realized that weeks had gone by without pain

long ago she had marched me ahead of her
with a maternal mission to execute
to the shop of Ned Wynne the shoemaker
where my wayward feet would find their truth

the man they never called "cobbler" looked down
at one five to noon and the other ten after
and all I could see was his bushy-eyed frown
'til his big hand stretched for a box marked 'inserts'

"there" he said as all the furrows ungathered
"ten past ten like the Town Hall clock
the image of your father and grandfather
and as good a dancer now no doubt"

Billy's Wife

they tell me there's no Guardian Angel anymore
does he now collect on Thursdays
or has he left for foreign shores

where are you Bridie
Christmas Eve and no candle in the window

the holly tree is heavy with red berries

where are you Bridie
Christmas morn and no fire lit

the mallard have long taken to the turloughs

where are you Bridie
the Wren Boys are calling sweet outside

the salmon are sheltering in the streams

where are you Bridie
New Year's Day and the calendar unchanged

the kingfisher would have known the humor of his friend

Pollard

it was only when the flock in our woods
expanded to seven
that the coins all began to drop
and I recalled that our grandmother used to
raise a rafter of seven each year to feed
each of the families at Christmas-
along with making seven plum puddings.

and out of that from the fog of memory
stepped the black-coated Miss Sylvester,
who we'd help cross the street
after she became blind from cataracts,
and the year her turkeys were found dead
under a blanket of feed before the Christmas market
where she'd hoped to sell them.

behind her was the outline of a vague
memory of the dance band she once led
and further back, just out of focus,
the name of the feed we used to sell her-
a name not verbalized for half a century
"pollard!"; and then the others we filled
into quarter, half and full stone bags,
depending on how much each customer
needed or could afford :
"pigmeal", linseed, bran and "amaizo".

wondering which animals these were fed to,
how many there were in each house,
where they were kept,
whether they were raised for consumption or sale,
I saw the faces of the only people
who could provide the answers

walking further and further away
into the fog, unable to hear me.
it felt as if they were heading back
into a time when the local grocer
made a difference in people's lives,
taking these and all the other answers
with them, forever.

Ballylinan

why they always referred to it
as having a harbor
I'll never know
-an oxymoron conjured up
by the same source that posed the
riddle "what's the difference between a duck"
or the notion that a person who failed to
declare himself a millionaire
would be sent to the dock?
for us it was the capital of conundrums
far from any sea with no river
running through it
and no still water
the proverbial "one horse town"
with Joe Nolan as saloon keeper
and his sister Hannah
late of New York as the femme fatale.
innocuous as cotton wool
it was perhaps a welcome antidote
to the scary stories we were told
about nearby Wolfhill
a place where small children might be sent
on misbehaving

small villages prove that
there is a relationship between
ignorance and innocence
as humans continue to demonstrate
a desire to kindle the
constant struggle
between the mundane and the absurd;
Ballylinan harbor and the world.

Climbing Into History

they sat side by side like retired stallions in Bapty's shed,
one whose engine hadn't started since the fifties
and wouldn't have been out of place in Capone's Chicago,
the other that had probably ferried the significants
of the Traveller community for half a century
behind four white horses to their final glory.

they said that in those days when he was tired
Bapty would retire and leave the running of the bar to his clientele.
this meant to us kids who climbed the wall into his yard
that there was no big stick to chase us off;
all we had to deal with were feral cats,
layered veils of ancient cobwebs and the odd bat.

whenever we felt like it, we were free to imagine
ourselves driving a stagecoach in the wild west
or behind the wheel of a gangster getaway car
as we sat in these two ancient transporters of the dead.
the rear compartments were off limits, not for lack of curiosity,
but knowing we had already climbed far enough into history.

Trainland

snaking along behind backyards
and factories without signboards
with no road signs or even accurate
place names for locational guidance,
they traverse an almost parallel universe.
the folk that live along the line can count time
by the rumble of dishware in cupboards
and early morning whistles
serve as an additional alarm;
they take it for granted that unnamed travelers
sequestered behind reflective glass are observing
their vegetable patches and outdoor toilets
and whatever scrap heaps they have not cleared.
it's a world more like the dark side of the moon
than anywhere on earth
which only train travelers
can observe- like the flip side of a coin
or a nation's underwear.

images flash by faster than thoughts:
mini-meadows with oval tracks worn through by dogs with ADD;
un-manned children's swings swaying in the wind;
the odd clothes line with long johns hanging like the carcass of a husband;
all shapes and sizes of galvanized sheds built for unknown purposes.

it's the side of the movie set the camera never sees
which the passenger shares an intimacy with
seeking out the same backyards on each trip
looking for new things like a movie fan
watching the same movie over and over
or a reader seeking new insights from a poem.

Black Babies

the late night cuddle-chats
that sowed the seeds of your father's best ideas
might have been the first form of hacking
in times before women escaped the cloak
of enforced subtlety
but for subliminal proselytizing
you couldn't beat the nuns.

after a half century I'm still tormented
by the never replicated taste
of whatever crusty bun
from the bakery down the town
they gave us in Senior Infants
for every big copper penny
we donated for "the black babies".

the nuns' message somehow
passed through our stomachs
to our parents minds at a time when
all we knew of Africa
was Tarzan and apes
and elephants and lions
and all we cared about was that penny.

a half century later
some of those black babies
have followed the copper
all the way to its very source
and now outnumber the nuns
while my nose is still hunting the world
for those warm crusty buns.

To Newbridge and Back

going to Newbridge for matches
Frank would strategize-
depending on the anticipated crowd size

and the volume of traffic from Athy-
at which side of the grounds to park
to engineer the quickest escape,

for first on his mind was getting back
before the wave of supporters
to open the doors of the pub.

as a man from the bicycle age,
he was an atlas of the many ways
of pedaling back and forth to Newbridge,

which for a distance of twenty miles,
is a virtual myriad more comparable
to that between some great capitals.

of course, from where we originated,
via Athgarvan made most sense
but that's where the logic ends,

for between Athgarvan and Athy
there must be a half dozen arterioles
that lead to the main Dublin road.

many times, Frank would take a fancy
to call in on the cousins in Nurney,
bringing into play The Curragh and Suncroft;

after that, we might take a right at Booleigh,
or go on through Fonstown and Kilmead
when he had something else to check out.

if there was any business in Kilcullen,
we 'd get a good stretch of the Dublin road,
which meant much of the trip could be in top gear.

some days, if the second game was boring,
we would head off looking for some holy well
or just roam the maze of roads in his beloved Kildare.

whenever there was a lull in the bar,
"what's the best way of going to Newbridge?"
could stir a debate for a good half hour.

Just Get on with It Man

and there he was
janowhaahmanelike
an East Hammer or
a Traveler on coke
making no sense
or a Corkman on crystal
jabbering on 'bout the North Mon
and the rebel yell and an' all that
janowhaahmanelike
and jackin' up in yer brain like
all fucked up
and goin' round 'n round man
in yer head with all stupid stuff
janowhaahmanelike
they're all the same
aren't they
even the yanks with their just-haircuts an' that
janowhaahmanelike
Sinead O'Connor
bishops and rabbis
and imams and that
goin' on and on
janowhaahmanelike
and the haris and lamas
and fahder this and fahder that
and the bishops
waste-ah-time man
janowhaahmanelike
I just get on with it meself
whatever I can like
put food on the table and that
that's all you can do like
when times are bad
janowhaahmanelike
just get on with it
janowhaahmanelike
just get on with it man

Measurers

when that temper takes control of your tongue
you lash at me that I'm "just a grocer's son"
and your temper is right
for I am still my father's son
and though most of the grocer has gone-
from the trade as much from me-
the measuring goes on

the sultanas, currents, raisins that we weighed
into quarter and half pound packs on Thursdays
the Guinness that we bottled into halves and pints
after the sugar and tea were done
and the bottles we washed endlessly
-having peeled off drunken slugs-
before packing into dozens

the smells of all are with me still
the sugar sacks with their mellow dryness
the black porter swilling round
and sickly sweet when spilt
the colors too of the dried fruits
the yellow, the red and the brown
against the white of the flour

the potatoes weighed in stones
on a larger scales
in the early morning
leaving scrapings of some farm undernail
and the smutty whiff of rot
from the meringue of a hollowed shell
which broke at your first touch

the rasping dryness of
coal and anthracite dust that were shoveled
into hundredweight measures
and the intoxicating fumes of paraffin
that would stay on our fingers long after
the gallons and half gallons were sold
and our black hands washed

yes I am a grocer's son
and if truth be known a son of
a son of a grocer's son
the last in a long line of measurers
whose days are largely done
though the measuring
still goes on

Garage Life

cadavers of Morrises and Austins all over the yard
from whose bones a renaissance vehicle would be created
-a mechanical Frankenstein for sale

after Jack had applied his mastery to the sheet metal
with one nostril on the paint jet
and a bandanaed Angela had manicured the interior

they would head to town for a quick pint
where half a half whiskey would be enough
to send Jack dancing over imaginary eggs

later in the evening we might see outside
their boss preparing for the night
with an adjustment in the rear-view mirror

of his latest toupee
above a three-in-one of aftershave
lip gloss and open collar

a ceremony designed with a single hope
of luring some young-one
into a quick oil change

Nemesis

we barely owned one LP between us
and were still in short pants;
the "app" was decades away
and "drugs" were just hearsay
(something that went on in America),
but The Square Pirates knew
every orchard for miles around
red , green or crab, apple or pear
and had climbed every roof
slate or galvanized
up to three stories high
and fought every troop of small boys
from this side of town to the "far side."

while we rode out on forays
the spinster Julia Mahon rode against us
to visit graves.

we knew the height of every wall
the presence of every hedge hole
and usually the bark of every dog.
we grew wary with experience
of houses with curtains pulled
or ones that had every fallen apple
already gather up,
but we were once surprised
by the choirmaster's wife
who had held her hound inside
until the moment a hand reached up
for a red delicious :
Mrs. Nevin was our nemesis

before innocence was lost
Julia Mahon rode against us
with equal force.

I call her out for she went so far
as to have the PP declare from the pulpit
that even contemplation of orchard robbing
was a mortal sin, for which
small boys would burn in hell.
for a short while we left it to
the Protestant members of the gang
to execute our plans
so that during confession
our souls could remain immaculate deceptions.
but in truth the start of Autumn term
was why the last of her apples were preserved
for Mrs. Nevin's tarts -and the birds.

after our innocence was lost
Julia Mahon still rode against us,
for hers was not.

The Coloring Book of a Young Nose

white is the smell of
sheets stripped from a clothesline
puffed with fresh air

gray is the smell of
benediction incense
around Eastertime

brown is the smell of
poor boys in and old shed
with their pants pulled down

red is the smell of
apples cut by my grandfather
with a worn penknife

black is the smell of
anthracite being shoveled
onto a weigh scales

green is the smell of
moss smearing your fingertips
as you climbed a wall

blue is the smell of
the fish market on Fridays
when Moore Street came down

yellow is the smell of
Gold Flakes and castor oil
old Uncle Edmond

mauve is the smell
of hydrogen peroxide on
knees in short pants

purple is the smell
of mother's face in May
under the lilacs

pink is the smell of
hives itching under blankets
calamine lotion

woodstain is the smell
of shopping before school term
Grafton Street Bewleys

sand is the smell of
sawdust and stale beer in pubs
that didn't mop out

blood is the smell of
the water from McStay's yard
where "fresh lamb" was made

snow is the smell of
the wallboard factory smoke
on northerly winds

ruby is the smell of
searching a handbag for coins
beneath her lipsticks

lime is the smell of
that wine gum no one wanted
in every packet

cream is the smell of
twice cooked lamb in shepherd's pie
straight from the oven

marble is the smell
of the fountain in the square
rank stagnant water

piebald is the smell
of canvas-topped caravans
and tinkers' horses

chocolate was the
musky damp smell in our hall
colors she hated

silver is the smell
of that pot she used just for
boiling potatoes

charcoal is the smell
of men sucking and blowing
bent pipes with black stems

teal is the smell of
a vest pulled up for mother
to apply Vicks' rub

lemon is the smell of
fear in the dean's office where
the bamboo cane fell

clear is the smell of
worms threaded onto a hook
and cast out for trout

orange is the smell of
Saturday wedding evidence
vomit on footpaths

blond is the smell of
a telephone booth at night
cheese and onion crisps

taupe is the smell of
a dead dog in the Barrow
sitting catching eels

lavender is the smell
of horse manure thrown on rose beds
beside her lupins

dark green is the smell
of my hated dinner day
bacon and cabbage

mahogany is the
smell of old rags with polish
the drawing room table

tan is the smell of
cattle dealers on mart day
with their shit-stained shoes

brass is the smell of
lucky bags from Nurse Candy's
an English thruppence

cherry is the smell
of sore throats and running noses
children's medicine

light green is the smell
of hard-boiled eggs being cut
to lay on lettuce

slate is the smell of
a mound of freshly dug soil
under a gravestone

plum is the smell
of roast chicken from the oven
wrapped with bacon strips

smokey is the smell
when fog mugged the chimneys
and choked the airflow

copper is the smell
of stains on fingers pulling
hard on Woodbine butts

olive is the smell
of ears clogged with wax
oil and cotton wool

mint is the smell of
lamb roasting in the oven
sauce table-ready

peach is the smell
of near-boiling Bird's custard
poured on the cold fruit

mustard is the smell
of sliced ham and tomatoes
spiced up by Coleman's

burgundy is the
smell of Kimberly biscuits
with your Ribena

amber is the smell of
Dwyer's Roscommon accent
on his whiskey breath

pastel is the smell
of sugar from bulk raisins/
currants/sultanas

beige is the smell of
Christmas when smoked hams were
stacked skin to skin

maroon is the smell
of Christmas cake just mixed
with glazed cherries

cinnamon is the
smell of brown paper torn off
Gran's plum pudding

turquoise is the smell
Enniscrone pier in July
mackerel everywhere

snow-white is the smell
of lime dashed onto stone walls
from whitewash buckets

coffee is the smell
of those truly cold days when
she would wear her furs

oak is the smell of
country boys with laced boots
sitting at school desks

creosote is the smell
of Hennessey's garage
with its oil-stained floors

rhubarb is the smell
of flour from pastry rolled
to make the pie crust

violet is the
smell of stained fingertips from
blackberry picking

rose is the smell of
rubber gloves wrapped 'round shears
mother pruning

crimson is the smell
of the small boy who was denied
"an bfhuil cead agam?"

treacle is the smell
of farmers in winter coats
supping Bovril

magenta is the
smell of boys with bare knees with
iodine spots

light brown is the smell
of mornings when the briquette
ashes were removed

scarlet is the smell
of dressing room muscle rub
before Athy games

off-white is the smell
of a dirty handkerchief
wiping a child's face

matt is the smell of
green dinosaurs with red eyes
crafted by crayons

gloss is the smell of
nothingness in cold season
daubs of Vaseline

tea is the smell of
watching birds from the small hole
in an empty chest

teak is the smell of
scary movies watched on chairs
treated for woodworm

dark is the smell of
paraffin stoves on Winter
days short as their wicks

warm is the smell of
newspaper with fish and chips
salt and vinegar

seaweed is the smell
of hot tea after rock fishing
socks and shoes drying

forty shades of green
is the smell of feet in boots
after pheasant hunts

yolk is the smell of
a sodden geansai soiled by
wild hens' rotten eggs

mackerel is the
smell of runners with light stripes
at night in dog shit

varnish is the smell
of church pews and Mah squinting
at unwashed armpits

pine is the smell of
the old man sawing quickly
into the soft planks

puce is the smell of
the lack of logic throwing
Jaye's fluid on vomit

cold is the smell of
the soft lungs of the mushroom
as your hand picks it

vapid is the smell
of the sins of a small child and
the confession box

color TV is
the smell of ice cream watching
the Munich World Cup

Technicolor is
the smell of cigarette smoke
after the pictures

eggshell is the smell
of whipped cream in meringues
bought from Bradbury's

metallic is the
smell of salmon in your bag
caught with a Stookie

ebony is the smell
of birds of no color
eating a carcass

ivory is the
smell of the dentist's mouth rinse
your shiny clean teeth

cheddar is the smell
of Coleman's mustard spread on
farmers' sandwiches

shiny is the smell
of leather shoes on Teddy Boys
below drainpipe pants

dull is the smell of
starch on St. Carmel's coif
a bride of Jesus

psychedelic is
the smell of the smoky rec-rooms
in the seventies

flame is the smell of
candle grease at Easter Mass
passing on the light

outrageous is the
smell of Mother's head shaking
feet in cheap high heels

wonderful is the
smell of the year's first rainbow
lamb roasting slowly

rainbow is the smell
of horses on the Curragh
the hats on Ladies Day

October is the
smell of singing taking out
moth balls from stored clothes

dreadful is the smell
of older girls in mini
skirts and cheap perfume

navy is the smell
of the gents' urinals
after the Harpic

honey is the smell
of sleepless summer evenings
the Scotch solution

autumn is the smell
of stewing sugar beet when
the south wind would blow

fuscia is the smell of
old photographs in a box
Kerry honeymoon

kaleidoscope is
the smells on market days from
so many counties

Our Peter Pan

it was all just a flutter wasn't it
a large bottle and a half of gin
down to Tralee for a monkey on the second race
and back to Frank's to one before the tea

hovering somewhere at the edge of our lives
you suddenly darted into the center of our every day
you were the mayfly to us

it was all just a flutter, wasn't it
a few quick ones before six Mass
over to Newbridge to see the mother
and back to Frank's before the bed

adopting us with your blanket of kindness
you warned us with a colorful cheeriness
you were the cherry blossom to us

it was all just a flutter wasn't it
a vodka and white before the dinner
up to Naas for a tip from the Super
and back to Frank's to see the race

You Are Not My Mother

an embedded ghost who has her touch and voice
you are not my mother
just some mischievous puppeteering poltergeist

you have come to test us with your thin disguise
skulking behind our loved one's eyes, you imposter
an embedded ghost who has her touch and voice

you removed her aches and pains but maintain her only vice
making sure a cigarette is always within her sight
you mischievous puppeteering poltergeist

she dives into sleep as the only means to fight
since you force her to relive every day as Monday
an embedded ghost who has her touch and voice

she was no performer of any type
it's your songs and rhymes coming from her mouth
mischievous puppeteering poltergeist

your quick half cups of black coffee don't fool us
Assam with milk in a China cup would be too refined for you
an embedded ghost who has her touch and voice

Small Town Sunrise

echoes of cock-crows skim down empty streets
large dogs do yoga with one eye on their shadowed silhouettes
a heavy truck rumbles in and rumbles out again
as the townsfolk roll over in their beds
small dogs head off somewhere on important business
cats slink home after a night chasing love
crows argue over a discarded burger supper
sparrows make busy as they eye the scraps
an angler in waders on a bike jousts with a long rod
old men carefully retrace the sidewalks they once skipped over
milkmen make faceless deposits outside shuttered shops
everything seems monadic and slow paced
until the sun chases the shadows off the streets
and quick as an earthquake
a cacophony begins
hall doors slam
birds feed in earnest
high heels slap pavements
children screech
engines rev
and the town roars itself awake

River Ukiyo-e

on days when the Barrow mimes a pond
and its surface is an inverted watercolor of bank life
and old Frank is talking about life before cars
before The Emergency (when the rest of the world was at war)
about how "the whole town lived on the river"
-a world his father thought would go on forever-
I think of that era as an ukiyo-e

men in waistcoats at the head of long boats
shouting instructions to children at the oars
here and there a plopping of divers
and the odd trout creating circles
teenagers swimming up and down
the bigger ones racing the men
others facing the blue skies lazily backstroking

I think of how his father never moved on
-how he still lived for the river
when other families had migrated to the roads
-how over his nine decades he never moved
from within a hundred meters of where he was born
-how a forth generation still rows
his business against contemporary currents

all along the banks women in flowery frocks
sitting on rugs with open picnic baskets
some bottle-feeding babies or dressing

younger children in bathing suits
some mothers wading in the shallows
with toddlers hanging from their arms
as cud-chewing Friesians observe from above

on those mime days I also think of my grandfather
lying in the parlor on his leather couch
now dependent on others for transportation
while the retired boat sits in the store outside.
I project through his closed eyes as he floats
down the river observing bank life like a swan
and a world he could not leave behind

here and there a swallow scoops a fly
odd crows loiter well back in the fields
waiting for a family to leave their rug
pet dogs bark and snarl at their wild cousins
and the odd stray cat that eases from the shade
of a big oak tree while sparrows dart all over
as an angler gently lays a line across a deep pool

Sixties Tattoo

on my left little finger
is a mark from the '60s
small and white
its statement is more in the memory
where every color is still vivid

it was applied by a black frocked man
with a sawed-off driver
like the old persimmon in my grandfather's set
that he picked with the care of
the seasoned pro he was
for its swing balance and polished shaft
and perfect woven grip
a man who always selected out "six for six"
at random
after his each of his absences from the room
to attend to his extra duties as headmaster

he would start at a slow pace
with a calm and steady build-up
but after the third round of six
he would work up an anger like a golfer
after that many double bogies
his entire tunic would become engaged
in the swing processes
like a main sail filling out
and the rest of the class would avert their eyes
in anticipation of the pain that was
about to be inflicted on the second three
whose identity was still unclear

in this century the news would have read
"a man was arraigned today for the alleged
systematic beating of young children

with a sawed-off Taylor Made R7;
he was taken into protective custody
after angry parents gathered outside his home"
and at the trial the jury would have learned that
he had carefully polished the cut shaft
to prevent splinters

back then the reality was that
for many boys the pain did not end at school
for the sight of their red throbbing
welted hands
would incite their fathers to add an extra whack
across the face
since whatever trouble they had surely caused at school
to deserve such punishment
had shamed the family
in "the sight of God"

little did we know that marks like ours
were the smallest
on the list of offenses committed by these
"men of cloth"
and that the colors of the tattoos
they left on others
had seeped into stains on their very souls
that can never be erased
and even after millions were spent
in guilt
they still will not admit
that they are not "Christian"
and were never "Brothers"

The Deliveries

in a time of mutual dependence
that widespread car ownership made obsolete
the delivering grocer
played a pivotal role in rural society

the first run was towards Monastervin
with stops on Stanhope Street and
on to Rathstewart
always with the same M.O. :
groceries on the kitchen table
and briquettes outside the back door
or -as we got further out of town-
maybe straight into a shed.
on the return we've veer towards Nurney
out the Geraldine Road
pausing in Prusselstown
at Johnny Connell The Tailor's house
often to drop off pants for the fitting of
a proper zipper
then steer back to cover
the estates off the Dublin road
ending up with an empty trailer half-way
to Castledermot.
at every stop the old man gathered
as much in news
as the amount of goods
I'd drop off.

"the far side" run was next
to Carbery's and up by Greenhills
snaking around St. John's Lane
past the CBS
then on to Barrack Street .
after a few drop-offs through
the pansy-lined front garden paths
along Pluman's terrace
it was onto the mystical Miss Mylods
whose ancient three story house was as bleak
as a scene from Wuthering Heights
and for whom our visit was a weekly highlight.
we'd end up in Parc Bride
the biggest blue collar estate
by which time we'd know exactly how
the main industries in the town were faring
and from the black eyes
how marriages were.

the southern run was more fun.
the first stop at the Miss Kellys
who the old man had convinced that
a daily bottle of stout promoted regularity.
(how a teetotal grocer got into such a
discussion with the trinity of spinsters
is an eternal mystery).
a few doors down was a Church of Ireland house
with a faded image of QE2 on the wall.
onward then to the Coneyboro bungalows
overlooking the Barrow
where stops at the Dunnes and Duffs would
be interspersed with skirmishes
with a posse of dogs for whom my father
kept a relic of his hurling days at the ready.
swinging back-handed through the door
as he steered with his left :
the Cuchulain of the Morris Oxford.

on then to Ardreigh
and Jimmy's cottage where the trapped smell
of boiled potatoes would engulf you
as you entered the front half-door
to drop briquettes near the hearth
careful to avoid tripping on the uneven dirt floor.
the entire experience was Dickensian
made worse when his wife ran off to England.
two miles down we would reach pure farmland
and a house with no electric light where
Paddy Loughman fended for himself.
neither his cats or their master
were properly domesticated
so bread and bacon stayed covered all day
under a large pot on the kitchen table.
after calls in Ballyroe and Grangemellon
our final stop was Levitstown
to the last of the farm laborers' cottages
bordering the Green estate
halfway to Maganey.
this was a long enough drive
to allow us to hear the racing results
and English league scores read in monotone :

"the three thirty at Fairyhouse-
Silly Old Lady two-to-one;
Plymouth Argyle 2, Aldershot 1;
Everton versus Man United postponed;"
and so on
and provided ten minutes of bonding
between a father and a son.

The Asbestos

those Athy men just went easy and slow
sipping pints and pulling long on Players
the languid Barrow makes her men mellow

grateful for the paycheck , they didn't know
every breath was laced with deadly fibers
those factory men just went easy and slow

flakes of toilet roll to stem the blood flow
he came early for his half of Powers
the languid Barrow makes her men mellow

clueless of the toll that was then unknown
he was proud to make sheets for the roofers
those factory men just went easy and slow

all my father said, "ah the poor fellow
sure he won't be a Christmas customer"
the languid Barrow makes her men mellow

pray for Jim Duff from the Coneyboro
that placid doomed man and all the other
Athy men who just went easy and slow
with the languid Barrow, far too mellow

The Traveler

an abandoned knife and fork
with hardening egg yolk stains
(that my mother would later curse)
sitting astride a half cut rasher
were telltale signs

a loud shout from the foot of the stairs
was another
(followed by a defeated sigh from herself)
"the Traveler's here"

and many years on
in spite or because of
the excitement of it all
I am now the one they could call
"the traveler"
with my honeybee's book of news
bouncing from country to country
with my bag of samples and open
order book
ready to tempt many good men away
from their wife's hot dinner
for a story and a pint of beer

The Barrow in Winter

In memory of Paddy Dillon, neighbor, lost to the river.

when the heron's legs on the weir
started to shorten,
we knew what was coming-
branches and full trees-
human garbage of all sorts-
often the stench of animals
kidnapped by the flood.
the weir decided whether
anything went on to Carlow
or just lingered in the dark waters
of the current-less canal.
once in a while,
a missing soul from Monasterevin
or from even closer to home,
would wash down
given to or taken by the river.
only the latter was ever recorded,
putting the blame on the Barrow
for our failure to look after our own.

The Dump

there was probably no other like in the country-
the custom-built delivery tow-trailer
the oulman had commissioned,
with flat ledges on either side for the easy unloading
and stacking of peat briquettes-
it was a true example of kaizen in its day.
every Thursday it served a different purpose
as the conveyor of rubbish to the town dump.
there were always small fires smoldering there
whose smoke combined with rotting food
to form a unique scent
which we'd bring home on our clothes.
besides the vermin, magpies and crows
and wild and half-wild canines,
there was always a dozen or so human scavengers
looking for their interpretation of "treasure"
in the discarded memories
and unwanted materials of others.
some weeks the oulman himself
transfigured into one of them and would
sanctify his discoveries by declaring
"now that could come in handy sometime!".
as a ruthless executioner of objects beyond their useful life,
his wife would never approve of the retrieved artifacts
and would "recycle" them the next week,
adding another concept to our vocabulary.
we eventually realized that the to and from the dump
had become part of the fabric of give and take
of which strong relationships are made-
just one more of the lessons learned growing up
from visits to the town dump.

www.ingramcontent.com/pod-product-compliance
Lightning Source LLC
LaVergne TN
LVHW090539110826
845146LV00003B/1178

* 9 7 9 8 8 9 9 9 0 4 5 7 8 *